I0559967

# HAPPINESS
## A JOURNEY TO JOYFUL LIVING

BY
O'BRIEN K. AWUAH

Email comments to the author at:
obrien371@yahoo.co.uk

ISBN:
Paperback: 978-1-967616-89-3
Hardcover: 978-1-967616-88-6

# Dedication

This book is dedicated to all readers who have found happiness in life despite its challenges. It is also lovingly dedicated to my amazing wife, Abigail Awuah, and our two wonderful sons, Ezekiel Awuah and Ethan Awuah.

# About the Author

O'Brien K. Awuah is a U.S. Air Force veteran, cybersecurity professional, and registered nurse with a deep passion for serving others. His unique background, spanning national defense, healthcare, and information security, allows him to bring a rich, multidimensional perspective to his writing.

He is also the founder of RHAFI Inc, a nonprofit organization dedicated to empowering individuals and communities through education, advocacy, and compassionate outreach.

Beyond his professional and philanthropic work, O'Brien is the author of several impactful titles, including The Immeasurable Mercy and Grace of God, Sorrow to Laughter, Tears of Mama Deya, and children's books such as Good Manners for Kids and Kijo, The Secret Celebrity. Whether exploring themes of faith, personal growth, or instilling values in young readers, his writing reflects a steadfast commitment to integrity, compassion, and purpose.

O'Brien continues to inspire readers of all ages with stories that uplift, educate, and transform.

# *Table of Contents*

# Individual Perspectives Of Happiness

Happiness is unique to each person. Your life experiences, upbringing, culture, religion, and economic status all play a role in shaping what happiness means to you. For me, sharing the gifts God has blessed me with, empowering others, and helping them recognize their worth fills me with joy. Knowing that I've made a difference in someone's life—that is happiness to me.

— *Ivette Diaz*

It is hard to define happiness in just a few sentences, but over the years, I've learned that happiness is deeply personal. For me, it's not about what I receive, but about the love I give and the presence I bring to each moment. Happiness is living fully in the now, finding joy in the small things—a flower in bloom, the song of a bird, the smile of a child. It's an attitude, not a destination—a way of moving through life with gratitude, peace, and hope, even when things don't go as planned. True happiness, I've discovered, comes from being at peace with myself and sharing love with others.

— *Carmen Medina Mercado*

To me, happiness is not found in the material things I have or even in what I think I want. Those things are fleeting and can be taken away in an instant. My joy comes from within. My joy comes from the Lord. If the Lord can see to the sparrow's needs, then He can certainly see to mine. My health, my family, my relationships, my walk with the Lord, the sunshine, the smell of salty air on the ocean breeze, the scent of fresh-cut grass and freshly baked bread, the special bond with my spouse, and the laughter of my children—these are just a few of the many things I cherish. When life becomes dark and the light feels harder to see, I turn to gratitude. I am deeply thankful for so many blessings.

I pray and seek support from those I trust. I lean on the wisdom of others. There is always something to be grateful for, even in life's most difficult times. We are truly never alone.

— *Kristen Earley*

Happiness is a personal experience unique to each individual. It is organically generated and shaped by one's life experiences. What brings happiness to one person may not resonate with another, and true happiness does not thrive on making others feel sad. In fact, happiness is contagious and has the power to uplift others from their misery.

— *Fredrick Osei Frimpong Jnr.*

To me, happiness goes beyond material things. True happiness isn't found in what you can hold in your hands—whether it's possessions, achievements, or status. It lies in the intangible moments that stir something profound within you—feelings and experiences that can't be measured or quantified. It's the kind of happiness that touches your soul, lingers in quiet moments, and leaves an imprint on your heart rather than just your senses.

— *Vivian Adu Gyamfi.*

Happiness is something you have to choose. Despite the good, the bad, and the ugly, you must choose to be happy, or you'll be swallowed whole by the darkness. Choosing the light is the only way to find happiness.

— *Capt Nicole Hendricks*

# Introduction

Welcome to *Happiness: A Journey to Joyful Living*, where we embark on a transformative exploration of what it truly means to live a life brimming with happiness and joy. In the hustle and bustle of modern life, amidst the trials and tribulations we face, the pursuit of happiness often seems elusive, like a distant dream just beyond our reach. Yet within each of us lies the innate capacity to experience profound joy and contentment, waiting to be awakened and unleashed. This book is not just a guide; it's a roadmap—a roadmap to discovering and nurturing the seeds of happiness that reside within you. Throughout these pages, we'll embark on a journey of self-discovery, exploring the depths of our hearts and minds to uncover the sources of true and lasting happiness.

But what is happiness, truly? Is it a fleeting moment of pleasure, a temporary state of euphoria? Or is it something deeper, more profound—a sense of fulfilment, peace, and purpose that permeates every aspect of our being? As we delve into the essence of happiness, we'll unravel its mysteries, debunk common misconceptions, and lay the groundwork for our journey ahead. Together, we'll explore the fundamental pillars of joyful living— cultivating a positive mindset, embracing self-compassion, nurturing meaningful relationships, finding fulfilment in daily life, overcoming obstacles, and practicing gratitude and mindfulness. Each chapter will be a stepping stone, guiding you closer to the radiant heart of happiness that beats within you.

So, are you prepared to start this adventure? Are you ready to unlock the boundless potential for joy and fulfilment that lies dormant within you? If so, then let us begin. Let us embark on

3

this odyssey of self-discovery, courageously charting a course toward a life filled with happiness, purpose, and unbridled joy. The journey awaits—let's take the first step together.

# Chapter One:
# The Pursuit Of Happiness

The pursuit of happiness is an intrinsic aspect of the human experience, a universal quest that transcends cultural, geographical, and socioeconomic boundaries. It is the relentless pursuit of that elusive state of being where joy, contentment, and fulfilment intersect. For many, happiness is synonymous with fleeting moments of pleasure or material wealth. Others mistake excitement for happiness. Both words are entirely different. True happiness extends far beyond the realm of momentary or material gratification. It is a deep-seated sense of well-being that emanates from living a life aligned with one's values, passions, and aspirations. It also refers to a profound, deep-seated joy or commitment that exceeds ordinary experiences of happiness.

The pursuit of happiness is not a destination but a journey—a journey marked by self-discovery, growth, and resilience. It is a journey of exploration, where we navigate the highs and lows of life, learn from our experiences, and evolve into the best versions of ourselves. At its core, the pursuit of happiness is about finding meaning and purpose in our lives. It involves cultivating meaningful relationships, pursuing our passions, contributing to the well-being of others, and embracing the beauty of the present moment.

Yet, the path to happiness is not always smooth or linear. It is full of obstacles, setbacks, and times of doubt. However, it is through adversity that we often discover our greatest strengths and resilience. I relocated to the United States in pursuit of better opportunities and a sense of peace in the land of promise. My journey was marked by challenges that hindered my success and happiness. I faced financial struggles and a wave of uncertainty. Graduating from nursing school was a battle, and passing the board exam presented yet another formidable obstacle. Joy seemed out of reach. Nevertheless, I persevered, applying every learning strategy I could and relying on the grace of God. Eventually, I achieved success and secured a nursing position at one of the healthcare centers in New York City. My heart overflowed with joy as my life transformed, bringing fulfilment through caring for patients.

Again, happiness means something unique to each individual and can be attained in various ways. For some, it may look like a life filled with constant joy, laughter, and the absence of pain or sorrow. However, the reality of life is different—it comes with challenges, hardships, and moments of uncertainty. The encouraging truth is that even in your darkest moments, you have the ability to cultivate happiness and inner peace.

God has placed a wellspring of peace within every person, empowering us to rise above life's uncertainties. For example, a mother grieving the loss of her child may find solace in dedicating her time to helping other grieving parents, transforming her sorrow into a mission of comfort and support. Similarly, someone battling a life-threatening illness might find inner peace by focusing on gratitude for the present moment, cherishing time with loved ones, and leaning on faith to find strength. These examples show that while life is not devoid of struggles, the ability to create peace within ourselves can transform those struggles into moments of growth and meaning.

Ultimately, the pursuit of happiness is a deeply personal journey—one that requires introspection, self-control, courage, and an unwavering commitment to living authentically. It is about embracing life's complexities, celebrating its joys, and finding beauty in its imperfections. As we embark on this journey, may we remember that happiness is not found in the destination but in the journey itself.

# The Concept of Happiness and Its Role in Our Lives

Happiness, the elusive yet universally sought-after state of being, is a concept deeply ingrained in the human experience. It transcends cultural boundaries, socioeconomic status, and individual differences, serving as a fundamental aspiration for people worldwide. At its essence, happiness encompasses a profound sense of well-being, contentment, and fulfilment in one's life. The value of happiness in our lives cannot be overstated. It serves as a guiding light, illuminating the path toward a life of meaning, purpose, and satisfaction, and it should have a positive impact on the people around us. Nearly each passing day, we hear news of vices in our communities that are beyond the control of our security agencies. Why these problems? Because some people have redefined happiness to gratify their personal desires. Truly, happiness should be deemed beyond mere pleasure or material wealth. It represents a holistic state of flourishing—an alignment of our innermost desires with our external circumstances.

When we experience happiness, we are more likely to cultivate positive relationships, pursue our passions, and contribute to the well-being of others. It fuels our motivation, creativity, and resilience in the face of adversity, empowering us to navigate life's challenges with grace and optimism. Moreover, happiness is not merely a personal pursuit; it has far-reaching implications for society as a whole. Societies that prioritize the well-being of their citizens tend to be more prosperous, cohesive, and resilient. By fostering environments that promote happiness and mental health, communities can unlock the full potential of their members, creating a ripple effect of positivity and fulfilment.

However, the pursuit of happiness is not without its complexities. In a world marked by uncertainty, stress, and societal pressures, achieving lasting happiness can feel like an elusive goal. Yet, it is precisely amidst life's trials and tribulations that the true essence of happiness reveals itself—not as a destination to be reached, but as a journey to be embraced. We will delve deeper into the multifaceted nature of happiness, exploring its various dimensions, debunking common myths, and uncovering practical strategies for cultivating joy and fulfilment in our lives.

## Misconceptions and Myths Surrounding Happiness

Happiness, often depicted as an idyllic state of perpetual bliss, is shrouded in misconceptions and myths that can obscure our understanding of what it truly entails. A common misconception is the notion that happiness is entirely tied to external factors like wealth, academic achievements, material possessions, such as mansions, luxury cars, and expensive clothing, or holding significant influence in society. While these can bring temporary satisfaction, they do not guarantee lasting happiness or inner peace. Research suggests that they only contribute to a fraction of our overall happiness. There are so many well-to-do people in our communities who are fond of displaying their wealth on social media to announce to the world how happy they are. However, the true state of happiness is revealed when they are alone or sleeping on their pillows. Those who use dubious means to acquire wealth are often watchful and filled with uncertainty. They express false happiness outwardly but live with constant fear.

Another common myth is the belief that happiness is a destination—a fixed point in the future that we must strive to reach. However, happiness is not a destination but a journey—a dynamic and ever-evolving process shaped by our thoughts, actions, and attitudes in the present moment.

Furthermore, there is a misconception that happiness is synonymous with the absence of negative emotions. In reality, happiness encompasses a broad spectrum of emotions, including sadness, anger, and fear. Embracing the full range of human emotions is essential for cultivating resilience, empathy, and emotional intelligence. Additionally, the pursuit of happiness is often equated with the relentless pursuit of pleasure and hedonistic indulgence. While pleasurable experiences can undoubtedly contribute to our happiness, lasting fulfilment is found in meaningful activities, meaningful relationships, and a sense of purpose that transcends momentary gratification.

Finally, there is a pervasive myth that happiness is a fixed trait—that some people are inherently happier than others and that happiness cannot be cultivated or developed. However, research in the field of positive psychology has shown that happiness is a skill that can be learned and through intentional effort, self-reflection, and mindfulness. By dispelling these misconceptions and myths, we can adopt a more nuanced understanding of happiness—one that empowers us to cultivate joy, resilience, and well-being in our lives, irrespective of external circumstances.

My grandmother, who is over a century old, cherishes the comfort of living in her old house rather than moving to a modern one in the village. For her, this home holds a lifetime of memories, as it is where she began her journey as a wife. It brings her immense joy and contentment to spend her remaining days in the very place that has witnessed her life's milestones and cherished moments. As we embark on this journey of exploration, let us challenge preconceived notions and embrace a holistic approach to happiness that honors the complexity of the human experience.

**Setting the Stage for a Transformative Journey Towards a Happier Life.**

Embarking on a transformative journey towards a happier life requires a deliberate commitment to self-discovery, growth, and change. It begins with a fundamental shift in mindset—a willingness to challenge old beliefs, embrace new perspectives, and open ourselves up to the possibility of transformation. At the heart of this journey lies the recognition that happiness is not merely a destination to be reached but a way of being—a conscious choice we make each day to cultivate joy, fulfilment, and meaning in our lives. It requires us to take ownership of our well-being, acknowledging that true happiness comes from within and cannot be solely dependent on external circumstances.

As we set the stage for this transformative journey, it is essential to cultivate a sense of curiosity and openness—a willingness to explore the depths of our hearts and minds, confront our fears and insecurities, and embrace the full spectrum of our human experience. It is through this process of self-exploration that we begin to uncover the barriers that may be hindering our happiness, whether they be limiting beliefs, negative thought patterns, or unhealed wounds from the past. Moreover, setting the stage for a happier life involves surrounding ourselves with support and encouragement, seeking out mentors, friends, and communities that uplift and inspire us on our journey. It also entails creating environments that nourish our well-being, cultivating habits and routines that promote physical health, emotional resilience, and mental clarity.

Above all, setting the stage for a transformative journey towards a happier life requires courage—the courage to step outside of our comfort zones, take risks, and embrace vulnerability in pursuit of our deepest desires. Many people find themselves trapped in misery, desperately longing to experience true happiness. Yet, they struggle to navigate the towering mountains of challenges and the deep valleys of hardships that stand in their way. Attaining true happiness demands unwavering sacrifice and a steadfast belief in oneself. It requires the courage to endure challenges, the determination to overcome obstacles, and the faith to keep moving forward despite life's uncertainties. It is a journey of self-discovery, growth, and self-empowerment— one that holds the potential to unleash our truest selves and unlock the boundless joy that resides within. As we stand on the threshold of this transformative journey, let us do so with an open heart and a steadfast resolve, knowing that the path to happiness is not always easy but is infinitely rewarding. Together, let us embark on this odyssey of self-discovery, embracing each moment with courage, curiosity, and an unwavering commitment to living our happiest, most authentic lives.

# Chapter Two:
# The Power Within

The power within is a profound force that resides deep within each of us, waiting to be awakened and unleashed. It is the essence of our truest selves—the source of our strength, resilience, and potential for growth. The power within is not bound by external circumstances or limitations but is boundless, infinite, and ever-present. At its core, the power within is rooted in self-awareness and self-empowerment—a deep understanding and acceptance of who we are and what we are capable of achieving. It is the recognition that we possess within us the innate ability to shape our destinies, overcome obstacles, and create the lives we envision.

The power within is also a catalyst for transformation—a catalyst that propels us forward on our journey of self-discovery and personal growth. It empowers us to break free from self-doubt, fear, and insecurity, and to embrace our fullest potential with courage and conviction. Moreover, the power within is a beacon of hope and inspiration—a reminder that no matter how challenging the circumstances may be, we always have the strength and resilience to persevere. It is a guiding light that illuminates the path ahead, showing us the way forward even in the darkest of times.

Ultimately, the power within is a testament to the limitless possibilities that lie dormant within each of us. It reminds us that we are not defined by our past, our circumstances, or our limitations but by the boundless potential that resides within us. As we embrace the power within, we unlock the key to living a life of purpose, passion, and fulfilment.

# Discovering the Inherent Power Within Ourselves to Create Our Own Happiness

Discovering the inherent power within ourselves to create our own happiness is a profound realization that can transform the way we perceive and experience life. It begins with the understanding that our happiness is not solely determined by external circumstances, but rather by the thoughts, beliefs, and actions we choose to cultivate within ourselves At the heart of this discovery lies the recognition that happiness is a choice—a conscious decision to focus on the positive aspects of life, to cultivate gratitude for the present moment, and to seek fulfilment in meaningful experiences and connections. It is an acknowledgment that we have the power to shape our own reality, to find joy in the simple pleasures of everyday life, and to create a life that resonates with our deepest values and aspirations.

Discovering our inherent power to create our own happiness also involves letting go of the belief that our happiness is dependent on external validation or approval from others. Instead, it invites us to turn inward—to cultivate self-love, self-compassion, and self-acceptance as the foundation for true and lasting fulfilment. Many people seek happiness through various social media platforms like Facebook, Instagram, TikTok, YouTube, and others. The comments and likes they receive on their posts often bring them a sense of satisfaction and validation, encouraging them to rely on their followers or subscribers for a feeling of happiness. However, this form of happiness is fleeting and superficial, as it depends on external approval rather than inner fulfilment.

Moreover, discovering the power within ourselves to create our own happiness empowers us to embrace resilience in the face of adversity, to find meaning and purpose in life's challenges, and to cultivate a sense of inner peace and contentment that

13

transcends external circumstances. Ultimately, the journey of discovering our inherent power to create our own happiness is a deeply personal and transformative one—one that invites us to reclaim our agency, to embrace our authenticity, and to live our lives with purpose, passion, and joy.

## Developing a Positive Mindset and Overcoming Restrictive Thoughts

Do negative thoughts hold you back from achieving your goals? You're not alone. We all encounter limiting beliefs—those insidious whispers that convince us we're "not good enough" or "doomed to fail." Fortunately, you can cultivate a positive mindset and break free from their grip.

➤ **Identify Your Limiting Beliefs:** The first step is recognizing those self-limiting thoughts. Are you constantly criticizing yourself? Do you shy away from challenges due to fear of failure? Take note of your inner monologue and spot any negative patterns that keep coming up.

➤ **Challenge Their Validity:** Just because a notion occurs to you doesn't make it accurate. Ask yourself: Is this based on evidence or fear? Are there successful people who share my perceived limitations? Challenge your beliefs with logic and counterexamples.

➤ **Reframe the Narrative:** Replace negative thoughts with empowering affirmations. Instead of saying, "I'm not good at public speaking," say, "I can learn and improve my communication skills." Focus on your potential and the progress you've already made.

➤ **Surround Yourself with Positivity**: Spend time with inspiring and motivating people. Avoid those who

14

reinforce your negativity. Seek out environments that nourish your growth and optimism.

➤ **Celebrate Small Wins:** Acknowledge and appreciate any advancement, no matter how tiny. This reinforces positive behavior and fuels your belief in your ability to succeed.

➤ **Visualize Success:** Spend time envisioning yourself reaching your goals. See yourself confident, capable, and victorious. This mental rehearsal strengthens your belief in your own potential.

➤ **Practice Gratitude:** Concentrating on your blessings shifts your viewpoint from one of scarcity to one of abundance. This fosters a positive mindset and opens you up to new possibilities.

Remember that developing a positive outlook is a journey, not a final goal. There will be setbacks, but with persistence and practice, you can break free from limiting beliefs and unleash your true potential. Embrace the challenge and unlock the incredible person you were meant to be.

## Embracing Gratitude and Mindfulness as Catalysts for Happiness

Embracing gratitude and mindfulness as catalysts for happiness unlocks profound avenues toward a more fulfilling and joyful life. Gratitude, the practice of acknowledging and appreciating the blessings and abundance in our lives, cultivates a mindset of richness and contentment. By focusing our attention on what we have rather than what we lack, gratitude fosters a sense of fulfilment that transcends material possessions or external achievements. It encourages us to savour the simple pleasures of life, to cherish moments of connection with loved ones, and to find beauty in the ordinary.

15

A young man, overwhelmed by life's struggles, decided to end his life. Before taking the drastic step, he removed his shirt and discarded it. As he prepared to carry out the act, he noticed another man eagerly picking up the discarded shirt and using it to cover his nakedness with gratitude and joy. This sight stopped him in his tracks. He ran to retrieve the shirt, realizing that, despite his struggles, he was still better off than others. It dawned on him that his life was worth living and that there was no need to give up. This story echoes the saying, "One man's meat is another man's poison." Many people often fail to recognize the blessings and opportunities they already possess. Instead, they focus on what they lack, feeling inadequate. True fulfilment comes when we appreciate what we have and understand that even in our struggles, others might see our lives as a source of hope.

Mindfulness, on the other hand, invites us to cultivate present-moment awareness and non-judgmental acceptance of our thoughts, emotions, and experiences. By bringing our attention to the here and now, mindfulness allows us to fully immerse ourselves in the richness of each moment, free from the distractions of past regrets or future anxieties. It enables us to experience life more fully, to savor the sensory details of our surroundings, and to cultivate a more profound sense of inner peace and tranquility.

Together, gratitude and mindfulness form a powerful synergy—a dynamic duo that amplifies our capacity for happiness and well-being. When we approach life with an attitude of gratitude, we naturally become more attuned to the present moment, more open to the beauty and wonder that surrounds us. Likewise, when we cultivate mindfulness, we deepen our capacity for gratitude, becoming more aware of the countless blessings and opportunities that enrich our lives each day. By embracing gratitude and mindfulness as catalysts for happiness, we tap into an infinite reservoir of joy and contentment that resides within us.

We learn to appreciate the richness of life's experiences, to find solace in moments of stillness, and to cultivate a profound sense of gratitude for the gift of existence itself. In doing so, we unlock the door to a life filled with meaning, purpose, and boundless possibility.

# Chapter Three:
# Embracing Change

Embracing change is a transformative journey that requires courage, adaptability, and a willingness to step outside our comfort zones. Change is an inevitable part of life—a constant force that shapes our experiences, challenges our assumptions, and propels us forward on the path of growth and evolution. At its core, embracing change is about surrendering to the ebb and flow of life, acknowledging that uncertainty and transformation are inherent aspects of the human experience. It involves letting go of the familiar and embracing the unknown, trusting in our ability to navigate the twists and turns of our journey with grace and resilience.

Embracing change also requires us to cultivate a mindset of curiosity and openness—a willingness to explore new possibilities, learn from our experiences, and embrace the opportunities for growth and self-discovery that change affords us. It invites us to release the grip of fear and resistance and instead approach change with a sense of curiosity, wonder, and excitement for the possibilities that lie ahead. Moreover, embracing change empowers us to break free from the constraints of our comfort zones and embrace the full spectrum of our potential. It encourages us to accept uncertainty as a catalyst for growth, to view challenges as opportunities for learning and expansion, and to cultivate resilience in the face of adversity.

At times, embracing change can feel like standing at the edge of a cliff, unsure whether the next step will lead to flight or freefall. Yet it is precisely in those moments of discomfort that we are offered the greatest opportunity for inner growth. When we allow ourselves to feel the fear without retreating from it, we cultivate a quiet strength that can only be forged through lived experience.

18

Change tests not only our adaptability but our capacity for hope and faith in ourselves.

After completing Officer Training School, I was assigned to Wright-Patterson Air Force Base in Dayton, Ohio. After twelve years in the Bronx, New York, leaving was a tough decision, as it meant parting ways with classmates, friends, and our church community. My wife and I faced significant anxiety and uncertainty about adapting to a new environment where we had no connections.

The first few weeks were particularly challenging. We struggled to secure permanent housing after utilizing the ten days of temporary on-base accommodation. Adding to the difficulty, my wife found it hard to navigate daily life with our kids when I was unavailable, as she deeply missed New York's extensive public transportation system that had enabled her independence without needing to drive.

However, things gradually improved. Once we moved into our own home and the kids started daycare, my wife began to feel more at ease. Over time, she came to appreciate the quieter life in Ohio—free from New York's massive traffic jams, high cost of living, and bustling crowds. It was a challenging transition, but it ultimately brought us a sense of relief and renewal.

Looking back, the upheaval forced us to confront aspects of ourselves we had long ignored. My wife discovered new layers of resilience and resourcefulness, and I learned to become more present and supportive in unfamiliar ways. We began to redefine what home meant—not as a physical location, but as a shared space of mutual trust, adaptability, and love. The shift wasn't only geographical; it was deeply internal, stretching and reshaping our sense of identity and belonging.

Ultimately, embracing change is a deeply transformative act—one that invites us to embrace the fullness of our humanity, to accept the impermanence of life, and to open ourselves to the endless possibilities for growth, evolution, and self-discovery that change brings. As we journey forward with courage and conviction, may we welcome change as a gateway to new beginnings, new adventures, and new horizons of possibility.

## Understanding the Inevitability of Change and Learning to Adapt

Change is an ever-present force in life—inevitable and relentless, like the tides. From personal milestones to global shifts, we encounter new realities often, sometimes welcomed, sometimes unwelcome. Resisting them can be exhausting, even futile. Instead, consider this: adaptability is your superpower. It's the ability to bend with the wind, navigate uncertainty, and emerge stronger. Here's why embracing change can unlock your full potential:

➢ **Growth Lies in New Experiences**: Each change, big or small, presents an opportunity. New skills, perspectives, and relationships blossom in unfamiliar territory. Think of it as mental and emotional fitness training—building resilience and flexibility.

➢ **Comfort Zones Can Become Cages:** Clinging to what's familiar can stifle your potential. Stepping outside your comfort zone, even if initially uncomfortable, can lead to unexpected discoveries and personal breakthroughs.

➢ **The Future Rewards the Adaptable:** Whether it's technological advancements or evolving social landscapes, the world around us is dynamic. Embracing change equips you to thrive in an ever-changing environment.

➢ **Uncertainty Can Be Your Friend:** It's tempting to fear the unknown. But uncertainty also holds opportunity. Embrace it as a chance to rewrite your story, explore new possibilities, and become the author of your future.

➢ **Growth Mindset is Key:** View each change as an opportunity to learn and grow. Believe in your ability to adapt, overcome challenges, and emerge stronger. This positive mindset becomes the fuel for your adaptability engine.

Remember, change is not the enemy. It's the constant that shapes us. By embracing it and honing your adaptability skills, you unlock a world of personal growth, resilience, and endless possibilities.

## Overcoming Fear of The Unknown and Embracing Opportunities for Growth

Overcoming fear of the unknown and embracing opportunities for growth is a courageous and transformative journey—one that invites us to step into the depths of uncertainty with an open heart and a resilient spirit. The fear of the unknown often stems from a natural human inclination to seek safety, security, and stability in familiar circumstances. However, it is in the face of uncertainty that our greatest opportunities for growth and self-discovery lie. To overcome the fear of the unknown, we must first recognize that uncertainty is an inevitable part of life— a natural and essential aspect of the human experience. Rather than viewing the unknown as a threat to be feared, we can choose to see it as a vast realm of possibility, ripe with opportunities for learning, exploration, and transformation.

Much of our fear stems not from the unknown itself, but from the stories we tell ourselves about what might go wrong. When we reframe uncertainty as a space of possibility rather than a pit of danger, we begin to shift our emotional posture. Perspective becomes our greatest tool. With the right lens, what once felt terrifying can become energizing. We stop asking, "What if I fail?" and begin to ask, "What might I become?" It's in this shift—from dread to curiosity—that growth becomes not just possible, but inevitable.

Embracing opportunities for growth requires us to cultivate a mindset of curiosity, courage, and resilience—a willingness to step outside our comfort zones, embrace new challenges, and lean into the discomfort of the unfamiliar. It involves trusting in our ability to navigate the twists and turns of our journey with grace and strength, knowing that each obstacle we encounter is an opportunity for learning and self-discovery. Moreover, embracing opportunities for growth invites us to release the grip of fear and resistance and instead approach life with a sense of openness, wonder, and excitement for the possibilities that lie ahead. It encourages us to embrace uncertainty as a catalyst for growth, to view challenges as opportunities for personal and spiritual expansion, and to cultivate resilience in the face of adversity.

Embracing growth doesn't require grand leaps into the unknown—it often begins with small, deliberate steps. Saying yes to a new experience, seeking help when we feel overwhelmed, or simply allowing ourselves to rest in uncertainty without needing immediate answers—these are all acts of quiet bravery. Over time, these small moments accumulate into a deep well of confidence and clarity. We realize that we're not just surviving uncertainty— we're evolving through it.

Ultimately, overcoming fear of the unknown and embracing opportunities for growth is a deeply transformative act—one that empowers us to step into the fullness of our potential, embrace the richness of life's experiences, and journey forward with courage, curiosity, and an unwavering commitment to personal and spiritual evolution. As we navigate the uncharted waters of the unknown, may we embrace each opportunity for growth as a precious gift, guiding us ever closer to the radiant truth of our being.

The journey through uncertainty and growth inevitably reshapes the external dimensions of our lives. Relationships evolve, careers pivot, and values deepen. What once seemed essential may fall away, making space for what truly matters. This isn't just internal transformation—it's the groundwork for a more aligned life. As we continue forward, the courage to face the unknown becomes a living compass, pointing us toward choices rooted in authenticity and trust.

## Finding Strength in Resilience and Flexibility

Life throws punches—sometimes gentle jabs, other times earth-shattering blows. It's easy to feel broken or defeated when faced with a financial crisis, job loss, the death of a loved one, divorce, sickness, or failure. But within us lies a hidden power: the ability to bounce back, stronger and more adaptable. This is the essence of resilience and flexibility, and it's the key to unlocking our true potential.

**Resilience** isn't just about surviving hardship. It's about emerging from it transformed. It's like the phoenix rising from the ashes—not unscathed but with the wisdom gained from overcoming adversity. Resilience allows us to bend without breaking, to weather the storm, and to emerge with newfound strength and a deeper understanding of ourselves.

**Flexibility** is the dance partner of resilience. It's the ability to adjust our sails to changing winds, navigate unexpected detours, and embrace alternative paths. It's not about abandoning goals but about adapting them to new realities. Flexible minds can see opportunities where rigid ones see only obstacles, turning challenges into stepping stones toward growth.

These two forces, working together, create an unbreakable inner core. Resilient and flexible individuals understand that change is inevitable, and they possess the inner tools to thrive in a constantly shifting world. They learn from setbacks, see opportunities in challenges, and adapt their course with grace and determination.

This can be likened to a flower being tossed back and forth by strong winds and rain. Despite the turmoil, its roots remain firmly anchored in the soil, drawing nourishment from deep within. Even under pressure, the flower seems to "smile," enduring the storm with quiet strength. Once the winds subside, it stands serene, ready for its regeneration of beauty and transformation. This is a powerful illustration of resilience and adaptability.

Here's how to tap into this inner strength:

➢ **Acknowledge your emotions:** Ignoring pain or fear won't make them disappear. Process them, learn from them, and let them go.

➢ **Focus on what you can control:** Not everything is in your hands, but your response always is. Choose to react with strength and resourcefulness.

➢ **Embrace a growth mindset:** Believe in your ability to learn and grow from challenges. See setbacks as opportunities to become a better version of yourself.

➢ **Develop a strong support system:** Surround yourself with individuals who uplift and inspire you—those who believe in your strength and resilience.

Remember, every scar tells a story of survival; every challenge overcome strengthens your resolve. By cultivating resilience and flexibility, you build an inner fortress that can withstand any storm. You become the architect of your own destiny, empowered to navigate life's journey with grace, strength, and an unwavering spirit.

# Chapter Four:
# Nurturing Relationships

Nurturing relationships is a cornerstone of a fulfilling and meaningful life. It involves cultivating deep connections with friends, family, romantic partners, and community members based on mutual respect, trust, and support. Nurturing relationships requires open communication, empathy, and a willingness to listen and understand the needs and perspectives of others. Investing time and effort into nurturing relationships can yield invaluable rewards, including emotional support, companionship, and a sense of belonging. Strong, healthy relationships provide a safe space where individuals can express themselves authentically, share their joys and sorrows, and celebrate milestones together.

To nurture relationships effectively, it's essential to prioritize quality time spent with loved ones—whether through shared activities, meaningful conversations, or simple moments of togetherness. Building trust and intimacy within relationships requires vulnerability and transparency, as well as a commitment to honesty and authenticity. Moreover, nurturing relationships involves showing appreciation and gratitude for the people in our lives, acknowledging their contributions, and expressing love and affection regularly. Small gestures of kindness and thoughtfulness can go a long way in strengthening the bonds of connection and fostering a sense of mutual care and respect.

Nurturing relationships isn't just about grand gestures—it's rooted in the everyday choices we make. It's in the check-in text sent just because, the undivided attention given during a conversation, or the decision to forgive even when it's difficult. These small, consistent acts build emotional trust over time. When we show up with presence, patience, and care, we signal to others that they matter—not just in times of crisis, but in the quiet, ordinary moments too. In this way, love becomes not just a feeling, but an active, daily practice.

Ultimately, nurturing relationships is an ongoing process that requires dedication, patience, and empathy. By investing in meaningful connections with others, we enrich our lives and create a supportive network of love and belonging that sustains us through life's challenges and triumphs.

## The Importance of Meaningful Connections in Fostering Happiness

Humans are social creatures, wired for connection. It's not just a feel-good perk—it's essential for our well-being and happiness. Strong, meaningful connections act as a safety net, a source of support, and a wellspring of joy, weaving a tapestry of fulfilment through life's ever-changing experiences. Beyond fleeting interactions, meaningful connections involve depth and understanding. They're built on shared experiences, vulnerability, and mutual respect. It's the laughter shared with close friends, the comfort of a listening ear during tough times, the celebration of each other's achievements, and the knowledge that no matter what, you're not alone.

These connections provide several key benefits:

➤ **Emotional Support:** Life throws curveballs. Knowing you have someone to lean on—who truly understands and cares—reduces stress and offers solace.

➤ **Sense of Belonging:** Being part of a community and feeling accepted and loved for who you are fosters a sense of security and well-being.

➤ **Increased Happiness:** Sharing positive experiences with loved ones amplifies joy, while their encouragement boosts your mood and overall outlook.

➤ **Enhanced Purpose:** Feeling connected to others gives life meaning and purpose. Knowing you contribute to someone else's well-being adds a deeper layer of fulfilment.

➤ **Stronger Health:** Social connections have been linked to lower blood pressure, stronger immune systems, and even a longer lifespan.

When we invest in meaningful relationships, we not only improve our own lives but also contribute to a more compassionate and connected world. One act of kindness, one moment of deep listening, or one sincere gesture can ripple outward—strengthening a relationship, inspiring someone else, or softening the edges of someone's day. These moments, though seemingly small, accumulate into the culture of a family, a community, or even a workplace. Connection, then, becomes both a source of personal fulfillment and a gift we offer to the world around us.

Cultivating meaningful connections isn't passive. It requires effort, vulnerability, and genuine interest in others. Take the initiative to reach out, actively listen, offer support, and be present in the moment. Remember, connections come in all shapes and sizes. Nurture relationships with family, friends, colleagues, and even online communities that share your interests. Every positive interaction adds a thread to the fabric of your happiness. In a world that can often feel isolating, prioritize building meaningful connections. They are not just a source of joy, but an investment in your overall well-being—and a key ingredient to a happier, more fulfilling life.

# Cultivating Empathy, Compassion, and Forgiveness in Our Relationships

Life is a dance of relationships—an intricate web woven with laughter, tears, and everything in between. But sometimes, the music falters, replaced by discord and hurt. That's when the three superpowers of empathy, compassion, and forgiveness step in, ready to restore harmony and heal the bumps along the way.

**Empathy** is the magical ability to step into another's shoes—to see the world through their eyes, even if it's different from your own. Imagine listening to a friend's heartbreak—not just hearing the words, but truly feeling the ache in their voice. It's the foundation of understanding, the bridge that connects hearts across differences.

**Compassion** takes empathy a step further. It's not just understanding; it's feeling with. It's the warm hug that says, "I see you, I hear you, and I care." It's offering a helping hand without expecting anything in return. Like sunshine nourishing a plant, compassion helps relationships blossom and thrive.

Now, let's talk about the elephant in the room: **forgiveness**. It's not about condoning wrongdoings, but about releasing the burden of anger and resentment. It's choosing to let go, not for the other person, but for your own peace of mind. It's like untangling a knotted rope, freeing yourself from emotional clutter, and making space for something better.

Sometimes, the hardest part of forgiveness or compassion isn't what others did—it's what we expected of them and didn't receive. The wounds from unmet expectations or emotional betrayal can run deep. In these moments, the practice of empathy may feel like a contradiction: how do you hold space for someone else's story when your own pain still echoes loudly? But the beauty of these superpowers is that they don't demand perfection—they invite presence. You don't need to feel completely healed to offer understanding. You just need to be willing to lean in, even if the effort is wobbly and unsure.

But let's be honest—cultivating these superpowers isn't always easy. It takes practice, patience, and sometimes, a healthy dose of self-reflection. Here are some pointers to get you going:

- **Listen actively**: Put away distractions, make eye contact, and genuinely try to understand the other person's perspective.

- **Challenge assumptions:** Don't jump to conclusions. Ask questions, seek their viewpoint, and avoid filling in the blanks with your own stories.

- **Offer kindness:** A small gesture, a listening ear, a gentle word—acts of kindness go a long way in fostering compassion.

- **Practice self-compassion**: Be kind to yourself, too. Acknowledge your mistakes and accept that everyone makes them.

- **Celebrate progress:** Small steps matter. Acknowledge your efforts and the growth you're making—both personally and in your relationships.

Remember, cultivating empathy, compassion, and forgiveness is a journey, not a destination. Bumps, disappointments, and periods of uncertainty are inevitable. But by embracing these superpowers, you'll not only strengthen your relationships but also create a more loving and understanding world for yourself and everyone around you. So go forth, embrace your inner hero, and start weaving a tapestry of connection that radiates kindness, understanding, and forgiveness!

Repair doesn't always come in grand reconciliations. Sometimes, it's a soft check-in after an argument. Other times, it's choosing to see the good in someone even when they're hard to love. The true strength of empathy, compassion, and forgiveness is that they offer us choices—to soften when we could harden, to stay curious when it would be easier to shut down. These moments of choice, taken again and again, quietly transform not just our relationships, but the people we become in them.

## Building a Support Network and Surrounding Ourselves with Positivity

Building a support network and surrounding ourselves with positivity are essential pillars of well-being and resilience in navigating life's challenges and triumphs. A support network consists of individuals who provide emotional, practical, and sometimes even spiritual support during times of need. These individuals can include friends, family members, mentors, colleagues, and community members who offer encouragement, empathy, and understanding. Creating a support network begins with fostering authentic connections and nurturing relationships built on trust, respect, and mutual care. It involves reaching out to others, sharing vulnerabilities, and being willing to offer support in return. By cultivating strong ties with individuals who uplift and inspire us, we create a safety net of love and support that sustains us through life's ups and downs.

Surrounding ourselves with positivity involves intentionally seeking out environments, activities, and people that foster optimism, gratitude, and joy. It means cultivating a mindset of abundance and possibility, even in the face of adversity. Whether through engaging in uplifting hobbies, practicing gratitude, or spending time with positive-minded individuals, surrounding ourselves with positivity empowers us to build resilience, deepen optimism, and nurture a lasting sense of well-being. Moreover, surrounding ourselves with positivity also entails setting healthy boundaries and limiting exposure to negative influences that drain our energy and dampen our spirits. By prioritizing our mental and emotional well-being, we create space for positivity to flourish and for our support network to thrive.

Building a support network and surrounding ourselves with positivity are transformative practices. They empower us to navigate life's challenges with grace, resilience, and hope. They remind us that we are not alone on our journey—and that together, we can weather any storm and celebrate life's joys with deeper meaning and connection.

# Chapter Five:
# Pursuing Passion And Purpose

Pursuing passion and purpose is a profoundly enriching journey that ignites the spark of inspiration and fulfilment within us. Passion is the fire that fuels our souls, propelling us towards the activities, interests, and endeavors that bring us immense joy, enthusiasm, and a sense of aliveness. It is the driving force behind creativity, innovation, and the pursuit of excellence in our chosen endeavors.

Purpose, on the other hand, is the guiding light that illuminates our path, infusing our actions and decisions with meaning, significance, and a sense of direction. It is the deeper why behind what we do—a reflection of our values, beliefs, and aspirations for a better world. When we align our passions with our purpose, we unlock a potent source of motivation, inspiration, and fulfilment. We become more fully engaged in our lives, experiencing a profound sense of resonance and authenticity in everything we do. Pursuing passion and purpose allows us to tap into our innate talents, strengths, and potential, empowering us to make a positive impact in our communities and beyond.

Moreover, the journey of pursuing passion and purpose is not without its challenges and obstacles. It requires courage, resilience, and a willingness to step outside our comfort zones in pursuit of our dreams. Yet, it is through overcoming these challenges that we discover the actual depth of our capabilities and the boundless potential that resides within us. Ultimately, the pursuit of passion and purpose is a transformative odyssey—a journey of self-discovery, growth, and self-actualization. It invites us to listen to the whispers of our hearts, to follow our intuition, and to embrace the fullness of our potential as we create lives filled with meaning, fulfilment, and joy.

The space between passion and purpose can sometimes feel like a wilderness—full of uncertainty, false starts, and quiet self-doubt. You may pour your energy into something you love, only to question its value or struggle to see how it contributes to the bigger picture. This is where many people falter—not because they lack desire, but because the clarity they crave doesn't arrive in a straight line. In these moments, it's vital to remain anchored in curiosity and grace. Allow yourself room to evolve. What feels foggy now often gains clarity in hindsight, as experiences layer upon each other and begin to reveal deeper meaning. Be patient with your journey. Trust that exploration is not wasted time, but the very soil in which purpose takes root.

## Determining Our Passions and Coordinating Them with Our Mission in Life

Ever felt like you're floating downstream, unsure of where the current will take you? Navigating life's journey can be tricky, especially when trying to reconcile what you love with what feels purposeful. But fret not, intrepid explorer! Finding the sweet spot between passion and purpose is possible, and it all starts with introspection.

### Step 1: Unearthing Your Passion Gems:

➢ **Dive into curiosity:** What sparks your joy? What activities leave you energized and engaged, even when faced with challenges? Jot down anything that sets your soul on fire, from hobbies to causes you care about.

➢ **Reflect on the past:** Think back to moments when you felt truly alive and fulfilled. What skills or activities were involved? Were you creating something, helping others, or simply exploring?

33

➤ **Challenge limiting beliefs:** Do you tell yourself, "I'm not good enough," or "That's not realistic"? Acknowledge these doubts, then counter them with evidence of your strengths and potential.

**Step 2: Aligning with Your Purposeful North Star:**

➤ **Connect the dots**: Look for common threads among your passions. Do they point towards a specific value you hold dear, a problem you long to solve, or a contribution you want to make?

➤ **Consider impact:** How do your passions intersect with the needs of your community or the world at large? Can you leverage your skills and interests to make a positive difference?

➤ **Embrace change:** Remember, your purpose might evolve over time. Stay open to learning, exploring new avenues, and adapting your path as you grow.

Remember, this is your unique journey. Don't compare yourself to others, and trust your inner compass. By uncovering your passions and aligning them with your purpose, you'll navigate life with intention, fulfilment, and the wind of joy at your back.

# Overcoming Challenges and Tenaciously Pursuing Our Goals

Life is a journey, not a stroll on a sunny beach. Obstacles rise like mountains, casting shadows of doubt and fear. But within us lies the spark of determination—a fiery resolve that whispers, "You can do this." It's this very determination that separates the dreamers from the doers, propelling us forward when the path seems bleak.

Obstacles are inevitable. They test our resilience, expose our weaknesses, and force us to dig deep. But remember: they are not roadblocks, but stepping stones. Every challenge overcome strengthens your resolve, hones your skills, and teaches valuable lessons. Embrace the power of "yet." When you hit a wall, don't say, "I can't." Instead, say, "I haven't learned how to do this yet." This simple shift in perspective opens doors to possibility, replacing defeat with the fuel of learning and growth.

Visualize your dream. Keep the image of your goal front and center. Let it illuminate your path, motivating you through setbacks and reminding you why you started. When doubt creeps in, revisit this vision—feel the fire of desire rekindle within. Remember, you're not alone. We all face challenges, even the most successful individuals. Seek out mentors, build a support network, and surround yourself with those who believe in you. Their encouragement and shared experiences can be a lifeline in the storm.

During challenging moments in my military career, I never faced the battles alone. My Christian faith served as a cornerstone, giving me hope and strength as I trusted God for relief. Thankfully, the military offers various resources, including Chaplaincy services and mental health support, which I utilized to maintain my resilience. Additionally, I was fortunate to have the unwavering support of my mentors and trusted leaders, who were always there to guide and assist me. Therefore, it is crucial not to isolate yourself in times of difficulty.

Celebrate small victories. Every step forward, no matter how seemingly insignificant, is a victory. Acknowledge your progress, reward yourself for your efforts, and let these celebrations fuel your resolve to keep going. Never give up. Determination is not a temporary burst of energy—it's the unwavering commitment to keep going, even when the going gets tough. Embrace the discomfort, learn from failures, and rise each time with renewed conviction.

Remember, the greatest stories are born from overcoming adversity. The dreams we achieve after conquering obstacles hold a deeper meaning and testify to the tenacity of the human spirit. So, don't let challenges deter you. Embrace the journey, harness the power of determination, and chase your dreams with unwavering zeal. The world awaits the brilliance you bring when you conquer and create!

And perhaps the most transformative reward isn't a finish line or public recognition—it's the quiet shift within. It's the resilience forged through trial, the confidence that comes from surviving what once seemed impossible, and the pride in showing up for your own dreams again and again. These victories may not always be visible, but they shape who you are becoming. Pursuing your passion and purpose is not just about what you achieve externally, but about the person you grow into in the process. That is the real triumph—the evolution of your spirit and the unshakable belief that your life has meaning, even when the world hasn't fully seen it yet.

## Finding Fulfilment Through Meaningful Contributions to the World

Finding fulfilment through meaningful contributions to the world is a noble pursuit that many individuals strive for. Here are some steps you can take to achieve this:

> **Reflect on Your Passions and Values:** Take some time to think about what matters most to you. Reflect on your passions, interests, and values. Which problems or causes truly speak to you? What kind of difference do you hope to bring about in the world?

36

➢ **Identify Your Strengths and Skills:** Consider your strengths, skills, and areas of expertise. What are you good at? How can you leverage your talents to contribute meaningfully to the world?

➢ **Set Meaningful Goals**: Once you have identified your passions and strengths, set meaningful goals that align with them. What specific contributions do you want to make? How do you see yourself making an impact?

➢ **Take Action**: Take proactive measures to fulfil your objectives. This might involve volunteering for a cause you care about, starting a project or initiative, or supporting existing organizations and movements.

➢ **Stay Committed and Persistent:** Making meaningful contributions to the world can be challenging and may require persistence and dedication. Maintain your commitment to your objectives in the face of obstacles or disappointments.

➢ **Collaborate with Others**: Collaboration can amplify the impact of your contributions. Seek out like-minded individuals and organizations to collaborate with. By working together, you can achieve more and make a greater difference in the world.

➢ **Celebrate Your Progress**: Take time to celebrate your progress and accomplishments along the way. Recognize the positive impact you are making, no matter how small it may seem.

➢ **Stay Open to Learning and Growth**: Remain open to learning and growth throughout your journey. Be willing to adapt and evolve as you gain new insights and experiences.

Remember, meaningful contributions to the world can take many forms—whether through activism, philanthropy, creative expression, scientific discovery, or simple acts of kindness and compassion in your daily life. What's important is that you find fulfillment in making a positive difference in the lives of others and in the world around you.

# Chapter Six:
# Mind, Body, And Spirit Connection

The mind-body-spirit connection represents the intricate interplay between our mental, physical, and spiritual dimensions, each influencing and shaping the others in profound ways.

Imagine a tree: the body is its sturdy trunk and roots, grounding us in the physical world; the mind is the branches, constantly reaching, analyzing, and processing the winds of life; the spirit is the sunlight and sky—intangible yet essential, guiding growth and providing purpose. When all three are in harmony, the tree flourishes—resilient, vibrant, and deeply rooted.

This holistic approach to well-being recognizes that optimal health and fulfilment arise from nurturing and balancing all aspects of our being.

The **mind** encompasses our thoughts, beliefs, emotions, and cognitive processes. It serves as the seat of our consciousness and the source of our perceptions and interpretations of the world around us. Cultivating a healthy mind involves practicing mindfulness, fostering self-awareness, and nurturing positive thought patterns. By encouraging our mental well-being, we enhance our ability to cope with stress, cultivate resilience, and promote a greater sense of clarity and inner peace.

The **body** refers to our physical vessel—the intricate network of cells, tissues, and organs that enables us to move, experience sensation, and interact with the world. Honoring the body involves nourishing it with nutritious foods, engaging in regular physical activity, and prioritizing rest. By caring for our physical health, we optimize our energy levels, enhance our vitality, and promote overall well-being.

The **spirit** encompasses our inner essence—the core of our being that transcends the limitations of the physical world. It encompasses our values, beliefs, and sense of purpose, as well as our connection to something greater than ourselves. Nurturing the spirit involves cultivating practices such as meditation, prayer, or spending time in nature that foster a sense of connection, meaning, and alignment with our deepest truths.

By recognizing and honoring the interconnectedness of mind, body, and spirit, we embark on a transformative journey toward holistic well-being and fulfillment. When we nurture each aspect of our being with care and intention, we create the conditions for greater harmony, balance, and vitality in our lives, allowing us to thrive and flourish on all levels of our existence.

## Nurturing Holistic Well-Being Through a Balanced Approach to Health

Nurturing holistic well-being through a balanced approach to health involves recognizing and addressing the interconnectedness of mind, body, and spirit in fostering overall wellness. It encompasses a comprehensive approach that integrates physical, mental, emotional, and spiritual dimensions of health to promote harmony and vitality.

A balanced approach to health begins with caring for the body through proper nutrition, regular exercise, and adequate rest. By nourishing the body with nutrient-dense foods, engaging in physical activity, and prioritizing restorative sleep, we optimize physical health and vitality. Additionally, nurturing holistic well-being involves tending to the mind by cultivating mindfulness, managing stress, and fostering positive thought patterns. Practices such as meditation, journaling, and mindfulness-based stress reduction techniques can help promote mental clarity, emotional resilience, and inner peace.

Furthermore, nurturing holistic well-being encompasses tending to the spirit—cultivating a sense of purpose, connection, and alignment with our deepest values and beliefs. Engaging in activities that nurture the spirit, such as spending time in nature, practicing gratitude, or participating in spiritual practices, can foster a sense of meaning and fulfilment in life.

By embracing a balanced approach to health that encompasses the mind, body, and spirit, we create the conditions for holistic well-being to flourish. Through intentional practices and mindful living, we cultivate resilience, vitality, and a profound sense of wholeness that enriches every aspect of our lives.

True well-being doesn't lie in perfecting each part in isolation, but in recognizing how they interact and inform one another. A peaceful mind can aid the healing body; a nourished body can open the door to spiritual clarity; a fulfilled spirit can bring balance to turbulent emotions. Holistic health is not a destination, but a continuous dance between awareness, alignment, and care across all dimensions of our being.

## Practicing Self-Care, Mindfulness, and Stress Management Techniques

Life's a whirlwind, and feeling overwhelmed is easy. But fear not, weary traveler! Taking care of yourself doesn't require hours of spa days. Simple self-care, mindfulness, and stress management techniques can be easily incorporated into your daily routine, bringing moments of calm amidst the chaos.

➤ **Self-care is your armor against stress.** Prioritize sleep, nourish your body with healthy food, and move your body in ways you enjoy. Even a five-minute walk or stretching session can work wonders.

41

➤ **Mindfulness is your superpower.** Breathe deeply a few times during the day. Focus on your senses: feel the breeze, listen to the birds, savor a bite of food. These mini-anchors bring you back to the present moment, grounding you amidst the worries.

➤ **Stress management is your toolkit.** When tension rises, try progressive muscle relaxation: tense and release different muscle groups, feeling the stress melt away. Deep breathing exercises help slow your heart rate and calm your mind.

Remember, **consistency is key**. Even small daily doses of self-care, mindfulness, and stress management make a big difference. Start with activities you enjoy and gradually integrate them into your routine. You'll be amazed at how these simple practices can transform your well-being, making you more resilient and ready to face life's challenges with a calmer, clearer mind.

## Cultivating Inner Peace and Harmony for Overall Happiness

Cultivating inner peace and harmony is a transformative journey that holds the key to overall happiness and well-being.

Imagine your inner world as a still lake. When the winds of stress, doubt, or distraction stir the surface, clarity fades. But when the waters are calm—when we cultivate peace and balance—we can see deeply, act wisely, and reflect our truest selves.

**Inner peace** is a state of tranquility and serenity that arises from a deep sense of acceptance, contentment, and alignment with our innermost selves. It involves cultivating a calm and centered presence amidst the busyness and chaos of daily life, allowing us to navigate challenges with grace and resilience.

**Harmony**, on the other hand, is the integration and balance of various aspects of our being—mind, body, and spirit. It involves aligning our thoughts, emotions, and actions with our core values and aspirations, fostering a sense of coherence and unity within ourselves and with the world around us. Cultivating inner peace and harmony requires intentional practices that nurture our inner landscape and cultivate a sense of connection to the present moment. Mindfulness meditation, deep breathing exercises, and yoga are powerful tools for cultivating inner peace by quieting the mind, reducing stress, and fostering a greater sense of awareness and presence.

Moreover, engaging in activities that nourish the soul, such as spending time in nature, practicing gratitude, or engaging in creative expression, can help cultivate a sense of harmony and wholeness within ourselves. By honoring our deepest needs and aspirations, we create the conditions for inner peace and harmony to flourish, paving the way for greater happiness, fulfillment, and well-being in our lives.

Begin with small steps—just a few moments of intentional breathing each day or a quiet walk in nature can create ripples of calm. Over time, these moments accumulate, shaping an inner sanctuary you can return to whenever life feels overwhelming.

Ultimately, cultivating inner peace and harmony is a lifelong journey—a continuous process of self-discovery, growth, and self-compassion. By nurturing our inner landscape with care and intention, we create the foundation for a life filled with joy, purpose, and meaning, allowing us to experience true happiness from the inside out.

# Chapter Seven:
# Gratitude And Joy

Gratitude and joy form a harmonious dance that enriches the tapestry of our lives with positivity and fulfilment.

Picture a quiet morning with a warm cup of tea in hand, sunlight spilling through the window, and a heart silently whispering thank you. In that stillness, gratitude blooms—and joy gently follows. These two emotions, when nurtured, create a harmony that enriches every moment of life.

**Gratitude**, a profound appreciation for the blessings—both big and small—that grace our existence, serves as a powerful catalyst for joy. When we cultivate gratitude, we shift our focus from what might be lacking to the abundance that surrounds us, fostering a sense of contentment and appreciation for the richness of our experiences.

**Joy**, the radiant emotion that emanates from a heart full of gratitude, is an effervescent celebration of life's moments, both ordinary and extraordinary. It is a deep-seated sense of delight that transcends circumstances, arising from an inner wellspring of positivity and appreciation. Together, gratitude and joy create a transformative synergy, uplifting our spirits and infusing our daily lives with a sense of wonder and fulfilment. Practicing gratitude opens our hearts to the beauty in each moment, while joy becomes the melody that accompanies our journey. Whether expressed through a simple thank you or experienced in the laughter shared with loved ones, this dynamic duo becomes a guiding force, shaping our perceptions and fostering a positive outlook on life.

We discover that even amidst challenges, there is always something to be thankful for, and in those moments of gratitude, joy blossoms, illuminating the path to a more meaningful and contented existence.

## Embracing the Practice of Gratitude as a Pathway to Joy

Like sunshine coaxing a flower to unfurl, the practice of gratitude can nurture joy within us, transforming our perspectives and enriching our lives. In a world often fixated on what we lack, cultivating an attitude of thankfulness allows us to appreciate the abundance already present. This shift, simple yet powerful, unlocks a pathway to greater happiness and fulfilment. Gratitude rewires our brains, fostering optimism and boosting positivity. When we acknowledge the good, we train our minds to seek it out, amplifying the positive moments and experiences. This heightened awareness allows us to savor the sweetness of a morning sunrise, the warmth of a loved one's embrace, or the quiet comfort of a good book. These seemingly small joys, often overlooked, become stepping stones on our journey to contentment.

Gratitude acts as a shield against negativity. By focusing on what we're thankful for, we diminish the power of complaints and grudges. This mental shift enables us to navigate challenges with resilience, identifying opportunities for growth even in the most difficult circumstances. Like a sturdy tree weathering a storm, a grateful heart remains anchored in optimism, even as life throws its curveballs.

The key to unlocking this transformative power lies in consistent practice. Start small: jot down three things you're grateful for each day, express appreciation to loved ones, or simply pause and savor a delicious meal. These mindful moments, like ripples in a pond, expand outward, creating a wave of positivity that touches all aspects of your life.

Remember, gratitude isn't about ignoring life's hardships; it's about acknowledging them while simultaneously cherishing the good. It's about choosing contentment over comparison and seeing opportunities for joy even in the midst of challenges. By embracing this practice, we open ourselves to the beauty and abundance that surrounds us, cultivating a heart that blooms with genuine and lasting joy. So, take a deep breath, appreciate the sunshine on your face, and embark on your own journey of gratitude. Remember, joy awaits around every corner, waiting to be discovered by a grateful heart.

## Finding Joy in the Present Moment and Appreciating Life's Simple Pleasures

Finding joy in the present moment and appreciating life's simple pleasures are transformative practices that invite us to slow down, savor the richness of each experience, and cultivate a deeper sense of contentment and fulfillment. In a world filled with constant distractions and busyness, embracing the present moment allows us to connect more fully with ourselves, others, and the world around us.

Whether it's basking in the warmth of the sun on a crisp autumn day, sipping a steaming cup of tea as rain patters against the window, or sharing a heartfelt conversation with a cherished friend, life's simple pleasures abound in the everyday moments that often go unnoticed. By cultivating mindfulness and presence, we become attuned to the beauty and wonder that surrounds us, finding joy in the small details and moments of grace that enrich our lives. It is in these simple pleasures that we discover a profound sense of gratitude and appreciation for the richness of our existence.

Moreover, finding joy in the present moment encourages us to release worries about the past and anxieties about the future, enabling us to fully immerse ourselves in the present moment. In doing so, we uncover a wellspring of inner peace and contentment that transcends external circumstances, anchoring us in the beauty and abundance of the present moment.

Ultimately, by embracing life's simple pleasures and finding joy in the present moment, we open ourselves up to a deeper, more meaningful experience of life, where every moment becomes an opportunity for gratitude, connection, and profound joy.

## Creating Daily Rituals to Cultivate a Mindset of Abundance and Positivity

Cultivating a mindset of abundance and positivity takes regular practice, and daily rituals can be powerful tools in this journey. To get you going, consider these suggestions:

**Morning:**

- **Gratitude Practice:** Start your day feeling thankful. Jot down three things you're grateful for in a journal, share them with a loved one, or simply take a moment to acknowledge them silently.

- **Positive Affirmations:** Repeat positive affirmations that resonate with you, like "I am worthy of abundance" or "Today will be a day filled with joy." Speak to them with conviction and believe in their power.

- **Visualization:** Take a few minutes to visualize your goals and dreams as if they are already coming true. See yourself achieving your aspirations and experiencing the emotions that come with success.

**Throughout the Day:**

- **Mindful Moments:** Throughout your day, take short mindfulness breaks. Focus on your breath, appreciate your surroundings, and acknowledge any positive emotions you experience.

- **Acts of Kindness:** Perform random acts of kindness for others, big or small. This could be something as simple as holding the door open, donating to a worthy cause, or offering a genuine compliment.

- **Celebrate Small Wins:** Don't wait for significant achievements to acknowledge your progress. Celebrate even the small victories and milestones along the way.

### Evening:

- **Reflection Journal:** Before bed, reflect on your day and write down three positive things that happened. Focus on the good, even if it was just a small moment of joy or a kind interaction.

- **Positive News Roundup:** Instead of dwelling on negativity, end your day by reading or listening to positive news stories. This will leave you feeling hopeful and inspired.

- **Spend Time in Nature:** Take a walk outside, even if it's just for a few minutes. Immersing yourself in nature can boost your mood and remind you of the world's abundance and beauty.

### Remember:

- **Consistency is key:** Don't get discouraged if you miss a day or two. Just pick yourself up and continue practicing.

- **Find what works for you:** Experiment with different rituals and see what resonates most with you.

- **Be patient:** Cultivating a new mindset takes time and dedication. Celebrate your progress and enjoy the journey!

- **Surround yourself with positivity:** Make a conscious effort to spend time with people who are positive and supportive.

- **Limit negativity:** Minimize exposure to negative news and people who drain your energy.

- **Help others:** When you help others, you not only bring joy to their lives but also cultivate a sense of abundance within yourself.

By incorporating these rituals into your daily routine, you can start cultivating a mindset of abundance and positivity, attracting more joy and fulfillment into your life. Remember, you deserve to live a life filled with happiness and gratitude!

# Chapter Eight:
# Overcoming Obstacles

Overcoming obstacles is an intrinsic part of the human experience—a journey marked by challenges, setbacks, and moments of triumph. Each obstacle we encounter presents an opportunity for growth, resilience, and self-discovery, empowering us to tap into our inner strength and navigate the complexities of life with courage and determination.

One of the key aspects of overcoming obstacles is cultivating a resilient mindset—one that embraces adversity as a natural part of the journey and views setbacks as opportunities for learning and growth. Rather than allowing obstacles to define us, we can choose to see them as stepping stones on the path to success, resilience, and personal fulfillment. Moreover, overcoming obstacles often requires perseverance and determination—qualities that enable us to stay focused on our goals and be resilient in the face of adversity. By maintaining a clear vision of what we hope to achieve and taking consistent action towards our objectives, we can overcome even the most formidable challenges.

Seeking support from others can be instrumental in overcoming obstacles. Whether it's leaning on friends and family for encouragement, seeking guidance from mentors or coaches, or connecting with a supportive community, surrounding ourselves with positive influences can help us maintain our resilience and motivation in the face of difficulty.

Overcoming obstacles is a transformative journey that calls upon us to dig deep, tap into our inner resources, and embrace the inherent challenges of life with courage, resilience, and unwavering determination. By viewing obstacles as opportunities for growth, cultivating a resilient mindset, and seeking support when needed, we can navigate life's challenges with grace and emerge stronger, wiser, and more empowered on the other side.

## Strategies for Overcoming Challenges and Setbacks on the Journey to Happiness

Overcoming challenges and setbacks on the journey to happiness requires resilience, determination, and a willingness to adapt and grow. Here are several strategies to help navigate obstacles and setbacks effectively:

➢ **Cultivate a Growth Mindset:** Embrace adversity as an opportunity for growth and learning. Adopting a growth mindset enables you to view setbacks as temporary and see them as opportunities to develop new skills and gain valuable insights.

➢ **Practice Self-Compassion:** Be kind to yourself when things get tough. Acknowledge your emotions and treat yourself with the same kindness and understanding you would offer to a friend facing similar challenges.

➢ **Set Realistic Goals:** Break more ambitious objectives into more manageable chunks. By setting realistic goals, you can maintain momentum and celebrate progress along the way, even in the face of setbacks.

➢ **Seek Support:** Reach out to friends, family members, mentors, or support groups for encouragement and guidance. Surrounding yourself with a supportive network can provide perspective, encouragement, and practical advice during challenging times.

➢ **Focus on Solutions:** Instead of dwelling on problems, focus on finding answers. Brainstorm alternative approaches, seek advice from others, and be open to trying new strategies to overcome obstacles.

➢ **Practice Resilience:** Cultivate resilience by developing practical coping skills and healthy strategies for managing stress. Engage in activities that promote emotional well-being, such as mindfulness, meditation, exercise, or creative expression.

➢ **Maintain Perspective:** Keep setbacks in perspective by focusing on the bigger picture. Remember that setbacks are a natural part of life's journey and often provide valuable lessons and opportunities for growth.

➢ **Celebrate Progress:** Recognize and celebrate the small successes and turning points. Recognize and acknowledge your achievements, no matter how small, and use them as motivation to keep moving forward.

By adopting these strategies and embracing a positive mindset, you can navigate challenges and setbacks on the journey to happiness with resilience, determination, and grace.

## Cultivating Resilience and Bouncing Back Stronger from Adversity

Cultivating resilience and bouncing back stronger from adversity is a transformative process that involves developing inner strength, adaptability, and a positive mindset. Here are some key strategies for cultivating resilience:

➢ **Develop a Growth Mindset:** Accept adversity as an opportunity for growth and learning. Adopting a growth mindset enables you to view setbacks as temporary and see them as opportunities to develop new skills and gain valuable insights.

➢ **Build Strong Relationships:** Cultivate supportive relationships with friends, family members, mentors, and colleagues. Having a strong support network provides emotional encouragement, practical advice, and a sense of belonging during difficult times.

➢ **Practice Self-Care:** Prioritize self-care activities that support your emotional, mental, and physical health. Engage in regular exercise, prioritize sleep, eat nutritious foods, and participate in activities that bring you joy and relaxation.

➢ **Develop Coping Skills:** Identify healthy coping mechanisms for managing stress and adversity. Practice mindfulness, engage in deep breathing exercises, journaling, or explore creative outlets to express your emotions and process difficult experiences.

➢ **Maintain Perspective:** Keep setbacks in perspective by focusing on the bigger picture. Remember that setbacks are a natural part of life's journey and often provide valuable lessons and opportunities for growth.

➢ **Set Realistic Goals:** Break more ambitious objectives into more manageable steps. By setting realistic goals, you can maintain momentum and celebrate progress along the way, even in the face of setbacks.

➢ **Learn from Adversity:** Reflect on past experiences of adversity and identify lessons learned. Utilize these insights to develop effective resilience strategies and enhance your ability to navigate future challenges.

➢ **Stay Flexible and Adapt:** Remain open to change and adaptability in the face of adversity. Be willing to adjust your approach, seek alternative solutions, and embrace new opportunities that may arise from setbacks.

By cultivating resilience and bouncing back stronger from adversity, you empower yourself to overcome challenges with courage, determination, and grace. Through self-awareness, support networks, and positive coping mechanisms, you can navigate life's ups and downs with resilience and emerge stronger and more resilient on the other side.

## Converting Challenges into Chances for Development and Education

Turning obstacles into opportunities for growth and learning is a transformative mindset that empowers individuals to navigate life's challenges with resilience and adaptability. Rather than viewing obstacles as insurmountable barriers, this approach encourages reframing setbacks as stepping stones toward personal and professional development. Obstacles often present valuable opportunities for self-discovery and growth.

By embracing challenges as catalysts for learning, individuals can uncover hidden strengths, develop new skills, and gain valuable insights into themselves and the world around them. Adversity invites individuals to step outside their comfort zones, confront limitations, and cultivate resilience in the face of uncertainty.

Moreover, overcoming obstacles fosters a sense of empowerment and self-efficacy. Each triumph over adversity reinforces the belief that individuals have the capacity to overcome challenges and achieve their goals. Through perseverance and determination, individuals can transform setbacks into springboards for success, leveraging newfound knowledge and experiences to propel themselves forward on their journey toward personal and professional fulfillment.

Ultimately, the ability to turn obstacles into opportunities for growth and learning is a testament to the human spirit's resilience. By embracing adversity with courage and an open mind, individuals can unlock their full potential, cultivate resilience, and emerge stronger, wiser, and more capable of facing life's challenges head-on.

# Chapter Nine:
# Living Authentically

Living authentically is a profound commitment to aligning our actions, values, and beliefs with our true selves. It involves embracing our unique identities, accepting our imperfections, and following our passions without fear of judgment or conformity. Authentic living requires courage, vulnerability, and a willingness to honor our inner truths, even when they diverge from societal expectations or norms.

When we live authentically, we cultivate deeper connections with ourselves and others, fostering relationships based on honesty, transparency, and mutual respect. Authenticity empowers us to express our thoughts, emotions, and aspirations truthfully, allowing us to live with integrity and purpose.

Living authentically enables us to navigate life's challenges with grace and resilience, knowing that our inner compass and values guide our actions. By embracing authenticity, we honor the uniqueness of our individual journeys and empower ourselves to live fully, authentically, and unapologetically.

## Accepting Genuineness and Leading Lives True to Who We Are

Embracing authenticity is like shedding a mask and stepping into the sunshine. It's about living by your own values, expressing your unique essence, and letting go of the pressure to conform to societal expectations. Imagine aligning your actions with your passions, letting your true colors shine, and connecting with others on a genuine level. That's the liberating power of authenticity.

But the journey isn't always easy. Fear of judgment, societal expectations, and ingrained habits can make us shrink back. Yet, the rewards are immense. Living authentically fosters self-confidence, cultivates deeper connections, and fuels a life filled with purpose and meaning.

So, how do you start? Begin with self-discovery. Explore your passions, values, and what truly sets you apart. Notice what lights you up and what feels inauthentic. Then, take small steps: express your opinions honestly, pursue hobbies you genuinely enjoy, and surround yourself with supportive people. Remember, authenticity is a muscle that strengthens with use. With courage and compassion, you can shed the mask and embrace the true, radiant you.

## Letting Go of Societal Expectations and Embracing Our Uniqueness

In a world saturated with prescribed paths and expectations, the call to embrace our uniqueness can feel like a rebellion. It's a decision to shed the borrowed skin of "shoulds" and "supposed-tos" and step into the vibrant tapestry of who we truly are. Letting go of societal expectations isn't about disregarding responsibility or abandoning others' needs; it's about carving out a space where your authenticity can blossom, enriching both you and your world.

Imagine this: instead of chasing the gilded cage of "success" defined by others, you pursue your own definition of fulfillment. Maybe it's the quiet joy of creating art, the thrill of adventure, or the deep satisfaction of helping others. When you let go of expectations, you unlock the door to passions and purpose that resonate with your very core.

The path won't be smooth. Doubt and fear, ingrained habits, and the pull of conformity can be powerful forces. But remember, every act of self-expression, every choice aligned with your values, is a victory. Start small: wear that outfit that makes you feel like a star, pursue that unconventional hobby, or simply say "no" to something that doesn't resonate. Remember, embracing your uniqueness isn't about isolation; it's about attracting genuine connections. When you shed the mask of expectations, you connect with others on a deeper level, fostering relationships built on shared values and mutual respect. You become a beacon of authenticity, inspiring others to do the same.

Letting go of societal expectations is a lifelong journey, not a destination. There will be stumbles and moments of doubt, but along the way, you'll discover a joy, a sense of purpose, and a connection to yourself that was always waiting to be unearthed. So take a deep breath, shed the expectations, and embrace the beautiful, unique tapestry that is you. The world needs your authentic light.

## Finding Freedom and Fulfilment in Being True to Who We Are

Finding freedom and fulfilment in being true to who we are is a powerful and inspiring pursuit. It's a journey of self-discovery, acceptance, and living in alignment with your values and desires. While the path can be challenging, the rewards are immense. Here are some important things to think about:

➤ **Self-awareness:** The first step is understanding yourself. What are your values, interests, strengths, and weaknesses? What makes you happy, and what makes you feel drained? Engaging in self-reflection, journaling, and exploring different experiences can help you uncover these truths.

➤ **Embracing authenticity:** Once you know yourself better, embrace your unique qualities and express them without fear of judgment. This includes your interests, talents, opinions, and even your quirks. Authenticity fosters genuine connections and allows you to live a life that resonates with your core self.

➤ **Breaking free from expectations:** Societal pressures and external expectations often cloud our vision. Learn to differentiate between what truly matters to you and what you feel obligated to do. Challenge limiting beliefs and dare to pursue your own path, even if it seems unconventional.

➤ **Living your values:** Aligning your actions with your deeply held beliefs creates a sense of purpose and integrity. What do you stand for? What kind of impact do you want to make on the world? Choose a path that allows you to express these values authentically.

➤ **Setting boundaries:** Saying "no" to things that don't align with your true self is crucial for protecting your energy and well-being. Learn to set healthy boundaries in your relationships, career, and personal life to create space for what truly matters.

➤ **Continuous growth:** Being true to yourself is not a one-time achievement but an ongoing process of self-discovery and evolution. Be open to learning, growing, and challenging yourself as you navigate life's experiences.

The journey toward being true to yourself is unique and personal. There will be challenges, doubts, and moments of uncertainty. But the more you embrace your authentic self and live with intention, the closer you get to experiencing true freedom and fulfilment.

# Chapter Ten:
# The Ripple Effect Of Happiness

The ripple effect of happiness is a phenomenon where the positive emotions and experiences of one individual spread outward, influencing the well-being of others and creating a chain reaction of joy and positivity. When someone experiences happiness—whether through acts of kindness, expressions of gratitude, or moments of joy—it radiates outward, touching the lives of those around them.

The ripple effect of happiness transcends boundaries, cultures, and languages, connecting individuals in a shared experience of joy and well-being. As happiness spreads from person to person, it creates a ripple effect that uplifts communities, fosters resilience, and strengthens social bonds.

Moreover, the ripple effect of happiness has far-reaching implications for collective well-being and societal change. By cultivating happiness and positivity in our own lives, we contribute to a ripple effect that extends beyond ourselves, shaping the world around us in meaningful and transformative ways. Through acts of kindness, compassion, and positivity, we have the power to create a ripple effect of happiness that touches hearts, transforms lives, and inspires positive change in the world.

## Understanding the Impact of Our Happiness on Ourselves and Others

Happiness: a word synonymous with sunshine, laughter, and warm fuzzies. But its impact goes far beyond mere cheer. Our happiness creates a symphony, resonating within ourselves and rippling outward to paint the world in brighter hues. Within, happiness plays a vibrant concerto. Studies show it strengthens our immune system, making us more resilient to physical and mental challenges. It sharpens our minds, enhancing focus and problem-solving skills. Like sunshine nurturing a seedling, happiness allows us to flourish, leading to a longer, healthier life.

This symphony doesn't play solo. Happiness transmits through social connections, a contagious melody enriching the lives of those around us. Positive interactions fostered by happiness build stronger relationships, where trust and support bloom. We collaborate more effectively, fostering a community spirit. Witnessing someone's joy becomes a shared melody, uplifting others and creating a virtuous cycle of positivity. But the symphony doesn't end there. Our happiness becomes a crescendo, impacting wider circles. Happy individuals contribute to a more supportive environment, building stronger communities. Reduced conflict becomes a harmonious refrain, as empathy and understanding take center stage. Innovation and progress blossom, fueled by the collective energy of shared joy.

The conductor of this symphony? You! While genetics play a part, we hold the baton of happiness. Practicing gratitude, nurturing relationships, pursuing passions, and helping others become instruments of joy. Remember, your happiness isn't just a personal melody; it's a powerful harmony enriching yourself and the world around you. So, pick up your instrument, maestro, and let the symphony of happiness begin!

## Spreading Kindness, Positivity, and Love to Create a Ripple Effect of Happiness

Spreading kindness, positivity, and love creates a ripple effect of happiness that touches the lives of those around us. Acts of kindness, no matter how small, have the power to brighten someone's day, lift their spirits, and inspire positive change. By extending a helping hand, offering words of encouragement, or simply sharing a smile, we can create connections and foster a sense of community and belonging.

Positivity is contagious, and when we approach life with optimism and gratitude, we uplift those around us and create an atmosphere of warmth and joy. Our words and actions have the power to inspire hope, resilience, and compassion, fostering a culture of kindness and empathy in our communities.

Love is the ultimate expression of our humanity, and when we lead with love in our interactions with others, we create a space for understanding, acceptance, and healing. Love transcends boundaries and unites us in a shared experience of connection and belonging, nurturing the seeds of happiness and fulfillment in our hearts and minds. Through spreading kindness, positivity, and love, we become catalysts for positive change, igniting a ripple effect of happiness that radiates outward and touches the lives of all those we encounter.

## Embracing Our Role as Agents of Change in Creating a Happier World

Embracing our role as agents of change empowers us to shape a happier world through our actions, attitudes, and choices. Each of us holds the power to make a positive impact, whether through acts of kindness, advocacy for social justice, or promoting environmental sustainability. By embracing our agency, we acknowledge the significance of our individual contributions to the collective well-being.

As agents of change, we strive to foster inclusivity, compassion, and understanding in our communities, challenging harmful norms and advocating for equality and justice for all. Through our words and actions, we inspire others to join us in creating a world where everyone can thrive and flourish.

Embracing our role as agents of change requires courage, determination, and a commitment to living in alignment with our values. By embracing empathy, compassion, and love, we can sow the seeds of positive change and cultivate a brighter, happier world for generations to come..

# Conclusion:
# Embracing Your Journey To Joy

*"Embracing Your Journey to Joy"* invites you to embark on a transformative exploration of self-discovery, fulfillment, and inner happiness. Through this empowering journey, you'll uncover the keys to unlocking your true potential and embracing the richness of life's experiences.

This book delves into the profound significance of living authentically, embracing challenges as opportunities for growth, and cultivating resilience in the face of adversity. By embracing your unique journey, you'll learn to navigate life's twists and turns with grace, courage, and an unwavering commitment to joy.

Drawing on insights from psychology, spirituality, and personal development, *"Embracing Your Journey to Joy"* offers practical tools, inspiring anecdotes, and reflective exercises to guide you on your path to happiness and fulfillment. Whether you're seeking greater meaning in your relationships, career, or personal growth, this book serves as a compassionate companion on your quest for joy and self-discovery.

Prepare to embark on a transformative odyssey—one that illuminates the beauty of your unique journey and empowers you to embrace life's infinite possibilities with open arms. Your journey to joy begins here.

## Reflecting on the Transformative Journey Towards Happiness

Reflecting on the transformative journey towards happiness invites us to delve deep into the intricate tapestry of our experiences, emotions, and aspirations. It is a journey marked by moments of clarity, resilience, and profound self-discovery—a journey that transcends the pursuit of fleeting pleasures and embraces the pursuit of enduring fulfillment and contentment. As we reflect on our path towards happiness, we acknowledge the myriad challenges, setbacks, and triumphs that have shaped our growth and evolution. Each obstacle we've encountered has been an opportunity for learning and self-reflection, inviting us to cultivate resilience, courage, and compassion in the face of adversity.

Moreover, the journey towards happiness is as much about the destination as it is about the process. It is about embracing the full spectrum of human experience—the highs and lows, joys and sorrows, triumphs and setbacks—as integral components of our personal growth and transformation. Through reflection, we gain insight into the values, beliefs, and aspirations that guide our journey towards happiness. We uncover the patterns and habits that either nourish or hinder our well-being, empowering us to make intentional choices that align with our deepest desires and aspirations.

Ultimately, reflecting on the transformative journey towards happiness is a deeply introspective and empowering process—a journey of self-discovery, growth, and self-actualization. It is a testament to the resilience of the human spirit, the power of vulnerability, and the profound capacity for love and joy that resides within each of us.

## Empowering Readers to Continue Cultivating Joy and Fulfilment in Their Lives

Empowering readers to continue cultivating joy and fulfillment in their lives is a transformative endeavor that invites them to embark on a journey of self-discovery and personal growth. By providing insightful guidance, practical tools, and heartfelt encouragement, readers are inspired to embrace their inherent potential and live authentically in alignment with their deepest desires and values.

Through the pages of insightful literature, readers are encouraged to explore the depths of their hearts and minds, uncovering the sources of true happiness and fulfillment that resonate deeply within their souls. They are invited to reflect on their experiences, challenges, and triumphs, gaining valuable insights into the paths that lead to lasting joy and contentment.

Moreover, empowering readers to cultivate joy and fulfillment involves nurturing a sense of agency and empowerment—the belief that they have the power to shape their own destinies and create the lives they envision. By fostering a growth mindset, encouraging resilience, and celebrating their progress along the way, readers are empowered to overcome obstacles and fully realize their potential.

The journey towards joy and fulfillment is a deeply personal and transformative one—a journey of self-discovery, resilience, and empowerment. By empowering readers to continue cultivating joy and fulfillment in their lives, we invite them to embark on a journey of endless possibility, growth, and self-actualization, where each moment becomes an opportunity for greater insight, connection, and fulfillment.

## Encouragement to Embrace Every Moment and Live Life to the Fullest, with Happiness as Our Guiding Light

Life dances by like a butterfly on the wind, ephemeral and fleeting. Yet, within each fleeting moment lies a universe of experiences waiting to be grasped. Don't let them flutter past unnoticed. Embrace them wholeheartedly!

Happiness, like a guiding star, should illuminate your path. It's not a destination, but a journey filled with laughter, connection, and growth. Seek it in the sunrise painting the sky, the melody in a bird's song, the warmth of a loved one's smile.

64

Celebrate the victories, big and small, and learn from the setbacks, for they too shape the tapestry of your existence.

Step outside your comfort zone. Fear might whisper doubts, but remember, courage often blooms in the most unexpected places. Explore new passions, embark on adventures, and connect with people who inspire you. Embrace the unknown, for it holds the potential for extraordinary discoveries.

Life is a precious gift, not a guarantee. Savor the simple pleasures: the sun on your face, the taste of a delicious meal, the joy of creating something beautiful. Be present in each moment, for the past is gone and the future uncertain. Let mindfulness be your compass, guiding you towards appreciating the present, flaws and all.

Remember, happiness is not the absence of struggles, but the ability to find joy amidst them. It's about cherishing the good, learning from the bad, and dancing through life with an open heart. So, hold happiness close, and let it guide you as you embrace every fleeting moment.

The End